The World of Plants

Fruits and Vegetables

Carrie Branigan
and Richard Dunne

FRANKLIN WATTS
LONDON•SYDNEY

This edition 2008

Franklin Watts
338 Euston Road, London NW1 3BH

Franklin Watts Australia
Level 17/207 Kent Street, Sydney, NSW 2000

Editor: Kate Newport
Art director: Jonathan Hair
Designer: Michael Leaman Design Partnership
Line illustrations by Jeremy Leaman
Consultant: Gill Matthews, non-fiction literacy consultant and Inset trainer

Picture credits:
Alamy: 14br. Nigel Cattlin/Holt Studios: front cover below, 11tl, 11bl, 12cl, 14cr, 16, 18, 19br, 21b, 22l, 22c, 22r, 23. Alan & Linda Detrick/Holt Studios: 10cl. Bob Gibbons/Holt Studios: 11cr. Goodshoot/Alamy: 14bl. Chinch Gryniewicz/Ecoscene: 12bl. Nick Hawkes/Ecoscene: 8. Willem Harnick/Holt Studios: 6, 7, 11br, 19tl, 20. Peter Landon/Ecoscene: 19tr. Rosie Mayer/Holt Studios: 23c. Sally Morgan/Ecoscene: 17tr, 24. Sea Spring Photos/Ecoscene: 10br, 23tl. Ivor Speed/Holt Studios: 10bl. Inga Spence/Holt Studios: 14cl, 15t, 15c. John Veltorn/Holt Studios: 21t. Peter Wilson/Holt Studios: 17tl.

All other photography by Ray Moller.

Picture research: Diana Morris.

A CIP catalogue record for this book
is available from the British Library.

ISBN 978 0 7496 8309 2

Printed in Malaysia

Franklin Watts is a division of Hachette Children's Books, an Hachette Livre UK Company.

Contents

Fruits and Vegetables

Fruits and **vegetables** are parts of plants. The fruits and vegetables we eat are very good for us.

We eat many different fruits and vegetables.

Look at the picture above, which do you think are fruits and which are vegetables?
Some foods we eat are not fruits or vegetables.
See if you can spot the odd one out.

These are the fruits.

These are the vegetables.

People often think that mushrooms are vegetables because they grow in the ground. This is wrong; they are another group of living things called **fungi**.

What Is a Fruit?

Fruits are the parts of a plant that have **seeds** inside them. Some fruits taste sweet.

◀ Apples grow on trees.

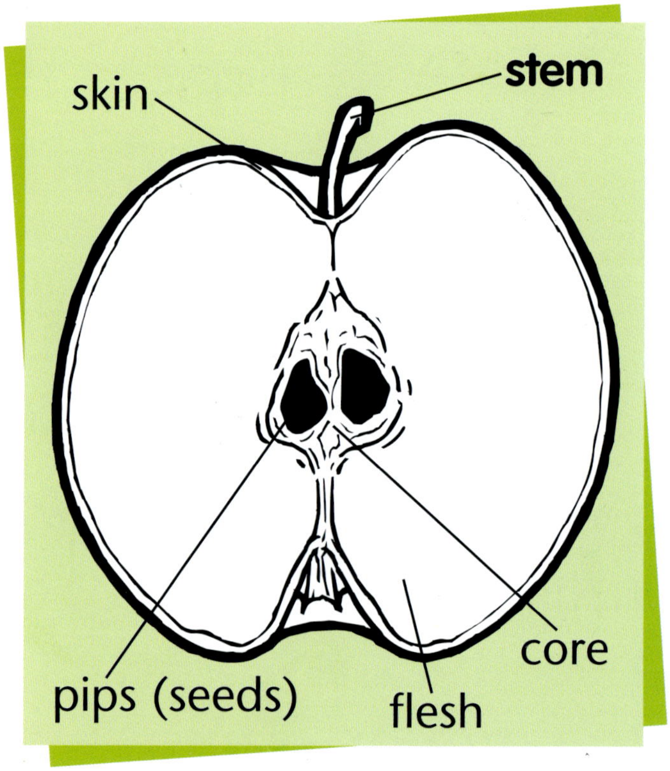

▶ If an apple is cut in half you can see the seeds. We call them **pips**.

We usually eat the **skin** and **flesh** of an apple but leave the core and pips.

Tomatoes are the fruits of a tomato plant.
When we eat tomatoes we eat the skin, the flesh and the seeds.

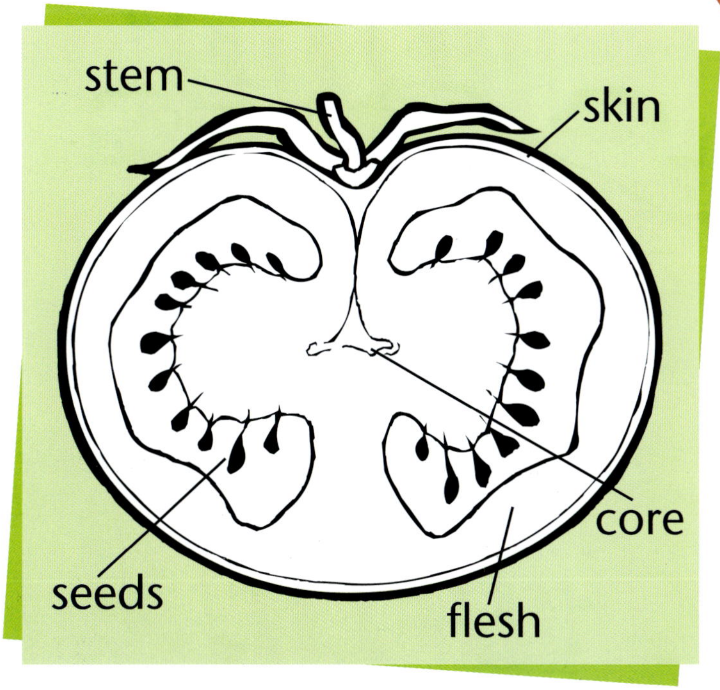

▲ This is a tomato. You can see the seeds inside.

▼ Here are some other sweet fruits that we eat.

Can you name these fruits?

Seeds We Can Eat

We eat **seeds** that grow inside **fruits**. Peas, beans and **nuts** are all seeds.

A pea **pod** is a fruit because it has seeds called peas inside.

◀ A pea plant with pea pods growing on it.

▶ Peas inside their pod.

▲ Beans are seeds. They grow inside a bean pod.

Nuts are seeds that are found inside a hard case called a **shell**. Peanuts and hazelnuts are seeds we can eat.

▼ Peanuts grow under the ground on a peanut plant.

▼ Hazelnuts grow on a hazelnut tree.

Can you name other seeds that we eat?

Grains Are Seeds

Wheat, oats, barley, maize, rice and rye are all **seeds** which are called **grain**. Grain is important because we need it to make many different foods.

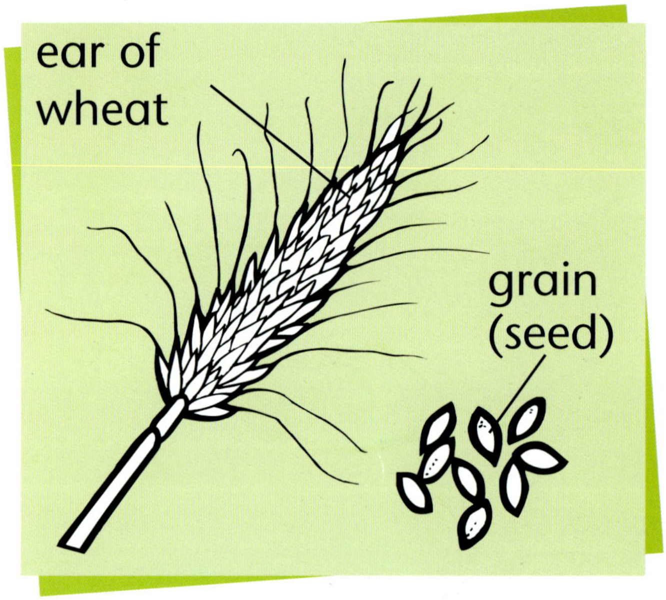

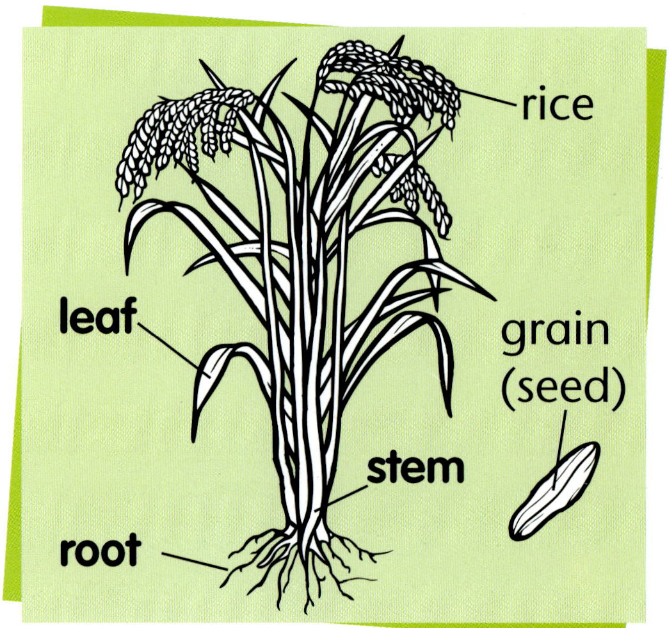

Bread is made from flour. Flour is made by grinding wheat or another grain into a fine powder.

▲ Look carefully at this bread and you can see the grains.

Breakfast cereals are made from lots of different types of grain.

Look at the list of ingredients on a cereal packet. How many different grains are there?

Dried Fruits

Some soft, fleshy **fruits** can be eaten when they are dried. Dried fruits are very useful because they last longer than fresh fruits.

When plums are dried, they become prunes.

When green grapes are dried, they become sultanas.

When black grapes are dried, they become raisins or currants.

Other dried fruits you can eat are apricots, figs and bananas. They are sometimes used in breakfast cereals and cakes.

A fruit cake contains many different types of dried fruits.

How many dried fruits can you find in a fruit cake?

Fruits and Seeds We Don't Eat

Some trees grow **fruits** that we can eat, like plums and peaches. Other trees have fruits and **seeds** that are too hard to eat.

We cannot eat the fruits of a sycamore tree.

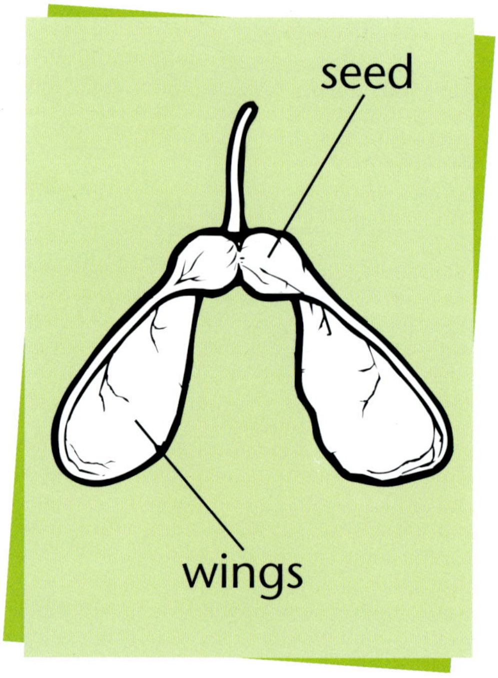

Sycamore tree fruits look like wings. When they fall from the tree they float and twirl down to the ground.

▲ The outside of a horse chestnut fruit is prickly.

The seed is very hard. ▶

▶ The fruit of a pine tree is a very hard **cone**.

Take a look at trees at the end of the summer and in the autumn. When do fruits fall off trees?

What Is a Vegetable?

The parts of a plant that are not **fruits** are **vegetables**. When we eat vegetables we are eating parts of a plant.

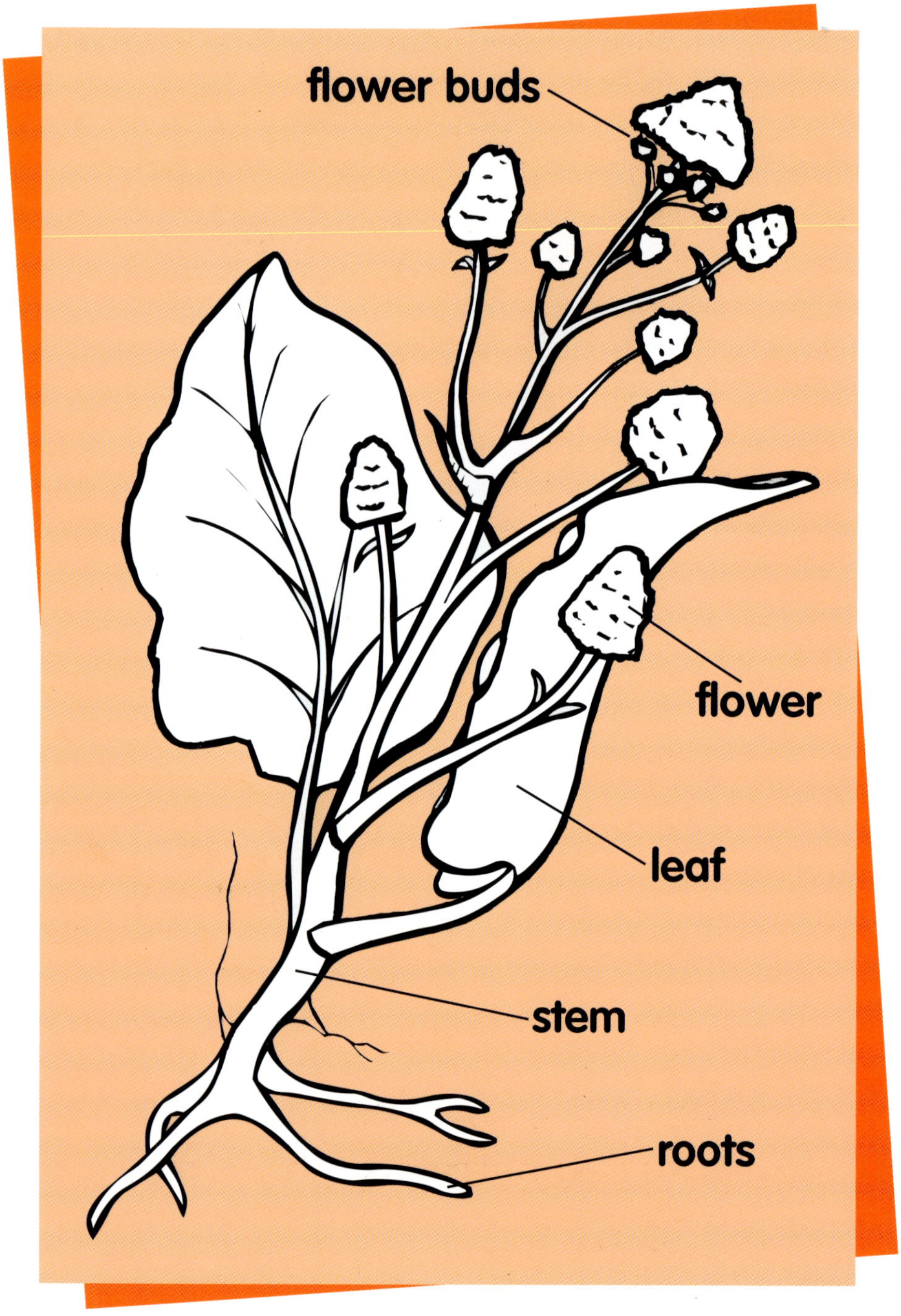

This drawing shows the different parts of sprouting broccoli.

See if you can work out which parts of these plants we eat. Do you know what the parts are called?

cauliflower

celery

spinach

parsnip

Visit the supermarket and look at all the vegetables. Try to work out which parts of the plants they come from.

Flowers and Stems

We can eat the **flowers** and **stems** of some plants.

When you eat cauliflower or broccoli you are eating the **flower buds**.

▶ A cauliflower

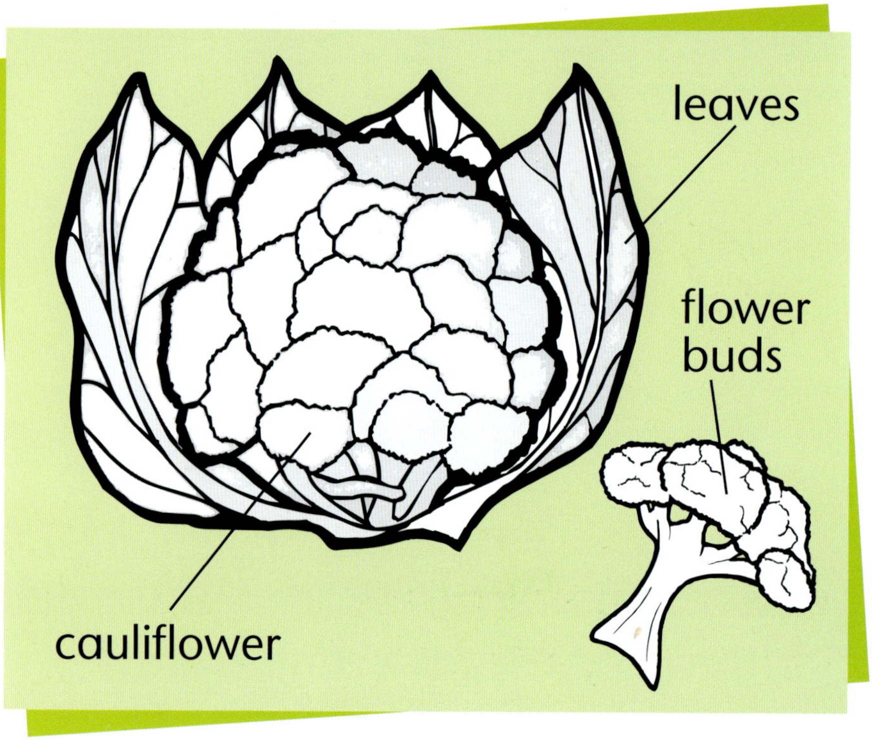

When you eat rhubarb you are eating the stem. We cannot eat the **leaves** as they are **poisonous**.

▲ Rhubarb

▼ Asparagus

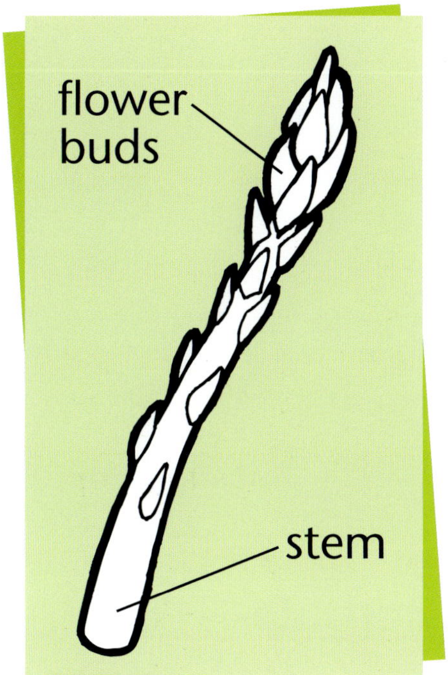

When you eat asparagus you are eating the stem and flower buds.

When you eat a leek, what part of the plant are you eating?

Leaves We Can Eat

We can eat the **leaves** of some plants.

Spinach

Red cabbage

Brussels sprouts

When you eat spinach, red cabbage and brussels sprouts, you are eating the leaves.

We eat lettuce leaves. Look carefully and you can see the **veins** on the leaves.

Have a look at some other leafy vegetables. Can you see the veins in their leaves?

Roots We Can Eat

We can eat the **roots** of some plants. Roots store food for the plant.

▲ Carrots

▲ Turnips

◀ When you eat carrots or turnips you are eating the root of the plant.

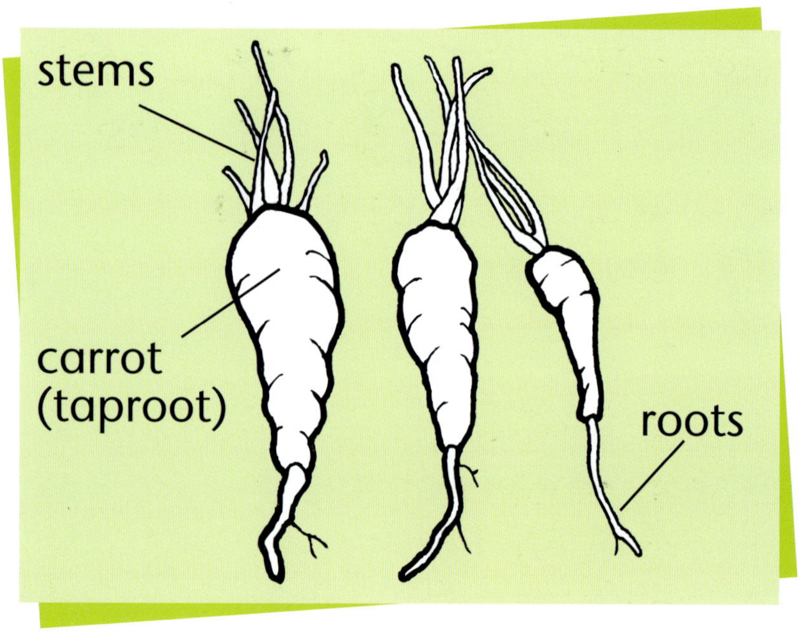

These vegetables are called **taproots**. They are the main root and have smaller roots coming off them.

▲ A potato plant.

People often think that potatoes are roots because they grow under the ground. In fact, potatoes are a type of swollen **stem**.

Have a look at a carrot or a turnip. Can you see where the stem of the vegetable was cut off?

Healthy Eating

Fruits and **vegetables** are good for us. We should try to eat at least five types a day.

▶ For breakfast you could eat some fruit on your cereal, such as a banana.

◀ For lunch you could eat a cheese sandwich with lettuce and tomato.

For dinner you could eat chicken, potatoes and beans.

For a snack you could eat a satsuma.

If you ate all this, you would have had six different types of fruits and vegetables.

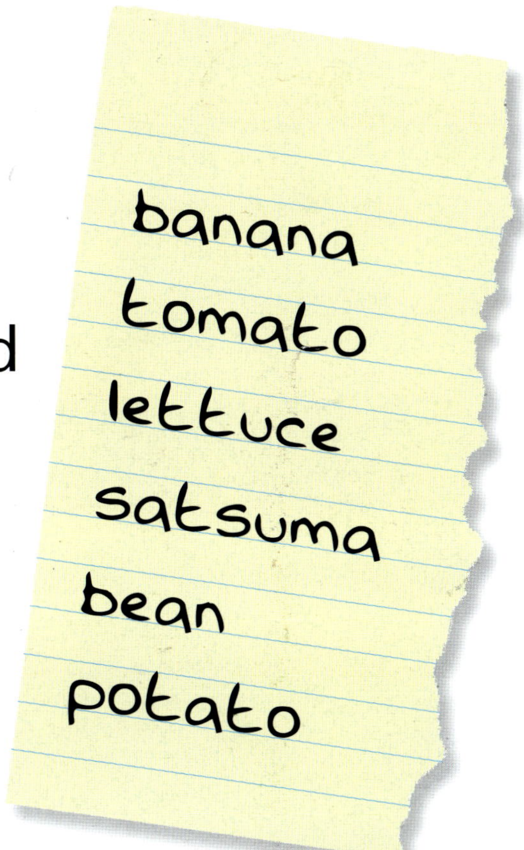

Which of these are fruits and which are vegetables?

Amazing Plants

- In 1984 a peach was grown in London, England, that was 30 cm wide. It was bigger than a football.
- The largest watermelon was grown in 1980 in Arkansas, USA. It weighed 90 kg – as much as a man.
- An enormous turnip was grown in Humberside, England in 1972. It weighed just over 16 kg – as much as a five-year-old child.

Use this book to find the answers to this Amazing Plants quiz!

- What are mushrooms?
- Can you name three types of sweet fruits?
- Where do peas grow?
- What is flour made from?
- What is a prune?
- On what tree would you find a conker?
- Where do potatoes grow?
- How many helpings of fruits and vegetables should you eat every day?

Glossary

cone type of fruit that is found on conifer trees.
flesh soft inner part of fruit or vegetable that we eat.
flower part of a plant that is usually very colourful. The flower becomes the fruit and seed of a plant.
flower buds flower before it is fully opened.
fruit part of a plant that grows from the flower and protects the seed or seeds.
fungi a group of living things including mushrooms, toadstools and yeast that grow on other living things. One of the group on its own is called a fungus.
grains cereal plants that are grown for foods.
leaf part of a plant that is usually green. The leaf uses sunlight, air and water to make food for the plant.
nuts fruits with hard shells that grow on some trees.
pips hard seeds in fruits.
pod type of fruit on some plants, such as bean and pea plants.
poisonous something that will make you ill if you eat or touch it.
root part of a plant that holds the plant in the soil. The roots take up water from the soil.
seed seeds are made in the flower of a flowering plant. When seeds are planted new plants grow from them.
shell hard casing that protects the seed.
skin outer covering of a fruit or vegetable.
stem part of a plant that holds up the leaves and flowers. The stem carries water from the roots to the leaves.
taproots main root of a plant with smaller roots growing off it.
vegetable part of a plant that is not the fruit, such as the flower, stem, leaf or root.
veins thin tubes in leaves that carry moisture around the plant.

Index